This Cycling Journal belongs to:

_____

Enjoy each moment of the ride.

Brought to you by Pennine Cycles

All content copyright© 2022 CST Creative Limited

After your first day of cycling, one dream is inevitable. A memory of motion lingers in the muscles of your legs, and round and round they seem to go. You ride through Dreamland on wonderful dream bicycles that change and grow.

- H.G. Wells

Enjoy the ride

I give myself time for ME. To ride and keep the **pedals** turning. It *doesn't matter* how often I do it, **THE IMPORTANT THING IS THAT I RIDE**. I push down on the pedals, FEEL THE WIND AROUND ME and go on an ADVENTURE. I ignore the voice inside **TELLING ME TO STOP OR SLOW DOWN**. Nothing beats the pure BLISS of riding my bike. It **makes me smile**. **The endorphins flow through my body**. *I feel like I can breathe*. I AM A PERSON WHO BELIEVES IN MYSELF. I am here to ride, to **enjoy** it and to do something that makes me *feel good*. Each ride is different even when it is the same. My HEART PUMPS, **my health is improving and I am getting fitter**. *I ride for my friends, my family and myself*. To give me a **happier** and **healthier** life. The most important part is that I always *enjoy the ride*.

Enjoy the ride & keep those pedals turning

How to use this
CYCLING JOURNAL

Cycling is the best activity in the world.

You're probably out there riding, week after week forgetting how far you've come and what you've achieved along the way. This is why we created the Cycling Journal. So you can record your rides. Whether it's your distance, how you felt or anything else cycling-related, this journal is a place for you. It's a chance to reflect, analyse and plan away from the screens of technology.

By recording your rides in this cycling journal you will be instantly more focused and closer to your cycling goals. Whether you are training for an event or race or for your own health and wellbeing.

Remember it's up to you to move towards your goals so keep your cycling journal close.

Have it in a place after each ride where you can easily access it and begin to see your progress over the weeks and months ahead.

The most important part of all is to **keep enjoying the ride**.

When the spirits are low, when the day appears dark, when work becomes monotonous, when hope hardly seems worth having, just mount a bicycle and go out for a spin down the road, without thought on anything but the ride you are taking.

- **Sir Arthur Conan Doyle**

www.ingramcontent.com/pod-product-compliance
Lightning Source LLC
Chambersburg PA
CBHW050243120526
44590CB00016B/2202